AF008474

When Stones Speak

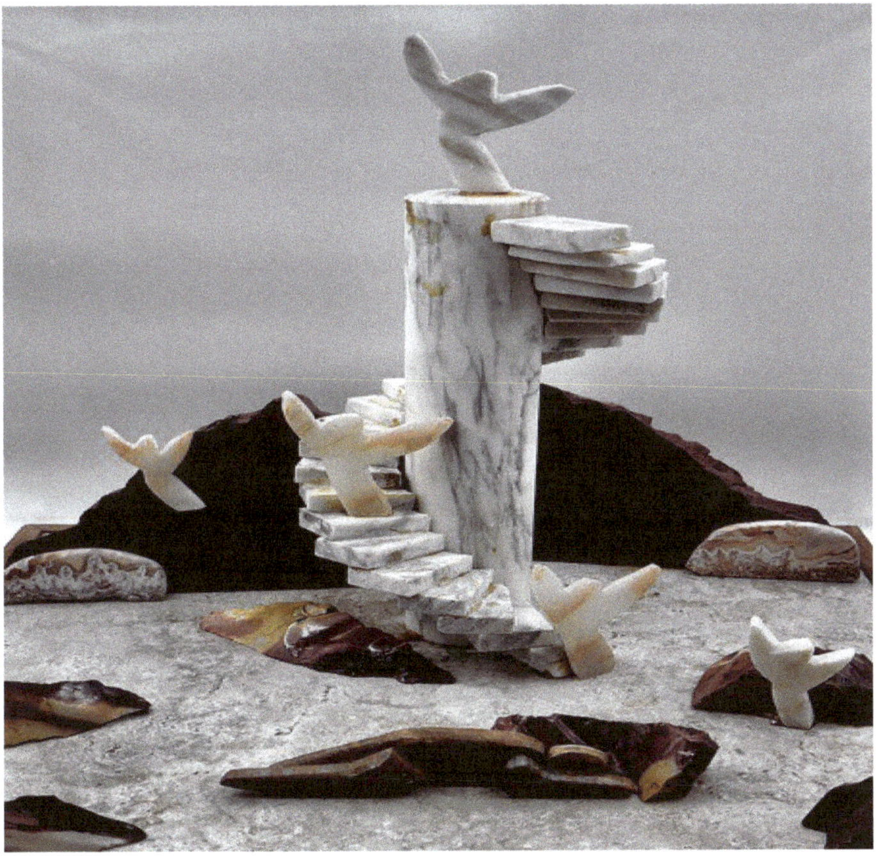

Stone Sculptures by Robert Watkins

Poems by Dwayne Cole

When Stones Speak
ISBN: Softcover 1-978-960326-59-1
Copyright © 2024 by Dwayne Cole and Robert Watkins

All rights reserved. No part of this book may be reproduced or transmitted in any form or by any means, electronic or mechanical, including photocopying, recording, or by any information storage and retrieval system, without permission in writing from the publisher.

Parson's Porch Books is an imprint of Parson's Porch & Company (PP&C) in Cleveland, Tennessee. PP&C is a self-funded charity which earns money by publishing books of noted authors, representing all genres. Its face and voice is **David Russell Tullock** who you can contact at: dtullock@parsonsporch.com.

Parson's Porch & Company *turns books into bread & milk* by sharing its profits with the poor.

www.parsonsporch.com

Dedication

This book is dedicated to all who appreciate art and want to see life with fresh new eyes.
Eyes that unite science and the humanities in a clear voice that brings healing
for our violent age. The end goal of biblical art, science, and the humanities is the same—
To express, beauty, truth, goodness, and peace in an adventurous healing spirit.

Welcome to—

      When Stones Speak
  Hear voices from unknown realms
        Rock of Ages

Preface

William Blake saw a world
in a grain of sand.

These sculptures and poems
go inside the stones to see
what centuries have hidden.

Sit with this stone art.
Feel God's tender love and care.
Receive the gift of Peace.

The stone poems,
go inside the stone sculptures
to explain the riddle of life—
Hidden through the ages.

Some stones were plucked from
river beds where rainbow trout came
and whispered secrets.

When picked up and sawed
sparks fly from them, so maybe
they contain light of stars.

Light to reveal the
Mystery of wisdom
written on walls of caves.
Etched in stone commandments.
Sun shining bright.
Star of Bethlehem!

Bible stone art teaches
the significance of life—
Jesus is Life.

Gentle Galilean Glories
Healing words of love.

The Glory of God
The Word made flesh
Heaven's Son Shine

As you meditate upon this art, may you come from scars of stones cast, to comfort of stone art, bowing in wonder. Let this be your prayer:

It is by the Goodness of God that I was born into this world in the first place. It is by the Grace of God that I am held every step that I take in life. And it is by the Love of God revealed in the gentle life and tender teachings of Jesus that I am becoming a child of God. Amen.

Introduction

As I viewed the beautiful stone work of Robert Watkins, each art work spoke to me, saying, "Write a poem about me." Stones are never isolated, but are connected with everything that is before them, beside them, under them, and over them. Stones both clothe and reveal the spirit of nature.
Stones have centuries compressed in them.

The interiority of a stone reveals itself for those who have eyes to see. Looking intently inside stones reveals the sparkle of lost stars.

A stone poem is nature magically revealing itself.

I often capitalize Beauty, Wonder, Tenderness, and Kindness as names for God. At a time when the name, God, is abused and associated with a conservative judgmental spirit, these stone sculptures and poems allow us to speak a fresh, inclusive, freeing message.

Most of the stone poems were written in the depth of Alaska's winters, a time of almost total darkness. This adventurous activity, created in me an invincible spring and summer. Photos and poems bring their own sunshine that warms our soul. Stones speak the magic of Wonder.

Robert Watkins is a stone mason,
sculpting the centuries, letting them speak.
No one knows where the stones came from—
Distant lunar stars or from the deep seas.
Stones preserve memory, the music of the spheres.
Stones speak silence and mystery.
Prehistoric animals howl in stones.
Time, sky, earth, and oceans sleep in stones.
Secret music of birds rest in stones.
Stones are precious, within them,
live diamonds and gold.
Dust of planets are inside—
Laughing in rubies.
When human language becomes inadequate,
Dwayne Cole creates poems
to let the stones speak.

Inspiring this book, *When Stones Speak*, are these scriptures—

As Jesus was riding into Jerusalem, the crowds were shouting praises to God. The Pharisees, however, are upset and ask Jesus to quieten them.

Jesus declares,

"I tell you,

if they were silent,

the stones would shout!"

(Luke 19:40)

Jesus is drawing on a powerful biblical precedent here of stones bearing witness to divine-human interaction and covenant (Gen. 28:17-18, Exodus 17:1-7, Numbers 20:1-13, Joshua 24:25-27).

A summary of these Old Testament rock stories is expressed in this Haibun:

Moses and the Rock of Sinai

In Exodus, chapter 17, we have this story:
The wandering people of God became thirsty
and complained to Moses saying, "Did you bring
us on this journey to die of thirst." Moses asked God
for help. God told him to take his walking stick and
strike the rock at Mount Sinai. Moses struck the rock
and water poured out for the people.

> Moses, we are thirsty.
> Moses struck the rock, stop, drink—
> Sparkling Life-giving water

Building on this miraculous rock imagery,
Matthew's Gospel says,

If the people of Jerusalem
won't recognize Jesus as the Messiah,
the stones of the city certainly will.
In Matthew's report of the cross, we read that as
Jesus breathed his last, the earth quaked
violently, and **rocks split** (Matthew 27:50-51).

How can they help but split,
when Jesus in whom all things hold together,
is broken on the cross?

Do stones speak?
Are they waiting to speak to us?
Most of the world says,
"No, no, it's not possible.
Stones can't speak."

If people were rocks,
I would like to be a stone mason.

Like Sisyphus, we rolled these stone sculptures and poems up the hill, seeking to let the light of heaven fall on them. Sometimes, they have just rolled down again. We kept rolling until the book was finished.

Now it is your time, friends,
to sit with them and let the
light of heaven fall on you.

Are stones delighted with their many colors, each one like a poem? This book of ekphrastic poetry, explores that question. Ekphrastic is a Greek word for poetry that is written about art. Ekphrastic poetry is art feeling itself.

>Gazing at stone art
>portraying tender teachings
>Jesus calms our soul

Ekphrastic poetry

meets stone sculptures—

Like meeting the Queen.

Bowing in awe and wonder,

you let stones speak first.

Poetry records the conversation.

Love flows. Be kind to all.

(For scriptures supporting the theme of kindness, see Appendices I and II at the end of this book.)

"Shepherds were in the fields near Bethlehem. They were taking turns watching their flock during the night. An angel from the Lord suddenly appeared to them. The glory of the Lord filled the area with light, and they were terrified. The angel said to them, 'Don't be afraid! I have good news for you, a message that will fill everyone with joy.'"
(Luke 2:8-10)

These stone manger scenes
give birth to heaven's angels
Messengers of love

Angel wings
Give birth to divine love
Glory of God

Stone angels
Cosmos from chaos
Glory to God

Manger miracle
From Mother Mary's womb
Birth of our Savior

Poet of universe
Comes to walk in our chaos
Cosmic love redeems

In stone art
Jesus the Living Word
Speaks tender words

Bible stone art teaches
Gentle Galilean Glories
Healing words of God

The Glory of God
The Word made flesh
Heaven's Son Shine

Stone art
Tender Jesus—
Mirror of Cosmos

Mirror confronting
what is actual
Disclosing what is possible

Stone sculptures and poems
take what is old and
turn it into something new

Silently listen to the stones
Hear them speak—
Shout good news

The sculptor has a view point

The poet has a view point

God the Poet is view

The birth of Jesus

Incarnation in stone art—

The Glory of God

I see the Manger

I don't understand it—But

I know what it's about!

Jacob's Ladder—

Prelude to New Testament and birth of Jesus

Fear not Jacob, You are Mine

Jacob fled from Esau.
Darkness descended.

The ground was his bed,
a **stone** was his pillow.

Jacob slept.
Heaven's door opened.

Jacob saw a ladder
reaching to heaven's throne.

In these awe inspiring moments—
Time stands still.

The world becomes so beautiful
our soul cracks open.

Letting the glory in!
Bright as the loving heart.

Come Jacob, into our wounded world.
Let love bring us out of darkness.

Teach us your patience, Jacob,
so we can climb Heaven's ladder.

Commune with the angels,
and inspire life with eternity.

Hope will not die!

Jonah was given a command to preach at Nineveh. He disobeyed. He boarded a ship to sail away from the presence of the Lord. During the time at sea a storm nearly sank the ship and Jonah was blamed for the storm because people found out about his disobedience to God's call. He was thrown into the sea to still the storm. He was swallowed by a whale, but was miraculously saved by God and given another chance to live a life of obedience.
(Paraphrase of Jonah 1:1-17)

I sit contemplating this sculpture
of Jonah and the whale. I remembered
A cloud shaped like Jonah's whale that I took
a few years ago. I had placed Jonah's words
on the whale and used the photo in my book,
The Bible: A Poetic Journey.

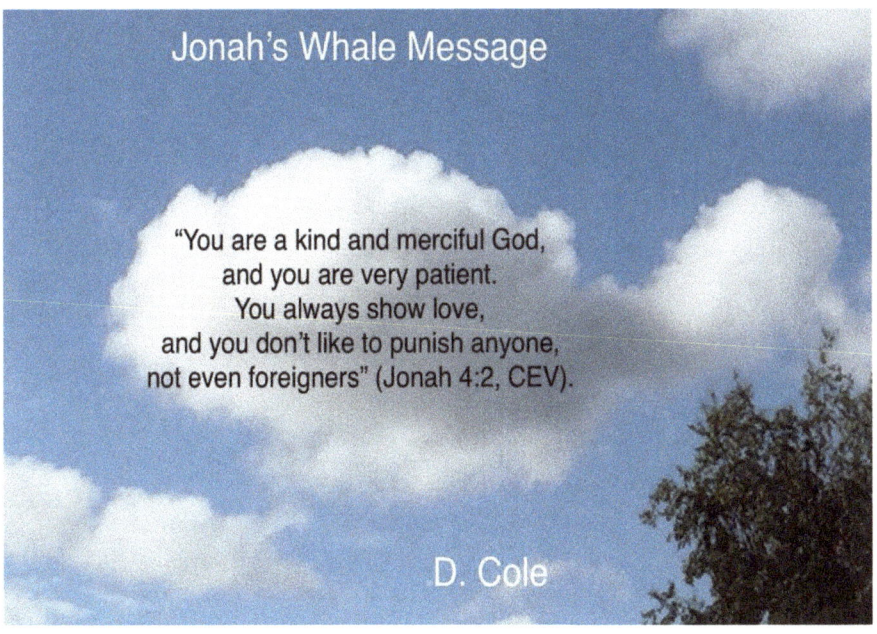

The words that I placed on the cloud photo
was the lesson Jonah learned from
being delivered from the whale.

Like Jonah, I reach out
for mercy and a little kindness.
As a child I was filled with light and joy.
Now dark questions abound,
injustice is seen all around.
Unkindness is the law of the land.
With Jonah let me learn:
"You are a kind and merciful God,
and you are very patient.
You always show love,
and you don't like to punish anyone,
not even foreigners." (Jonah 4:2, CEV)

I return from the cloud
a little more tender,
a little more loving.
Seeking to show
kindness to all.

Nativity Scenes

"Therefore the Lord himself will give you a sign: The virgin will conceive and give birth to a son and will call him Immanuel. (Isaiah 7:14)

The vision of these stone sculptures
and poems is grounded in beauty,
goodness, and adventurous love.
Come to this art and be soothed,
be healed. Find a new purpose
for your life.

This heavenly vision fuels
our optimism and hope for peace
in our world. Love that values
all persons and nurtures
the world soul in which
      We are all One.
        One in many,
         many in One.

Mary's Sonnet

While Mary was engaged to Joseph
of King David's family, an angel visited
Joseph and announced that Mary was
going to have a baby from the Holy Spirit.

You shall name him Jesus for he will
save his people from their sins. Mary said,
This is a surprise, am I to be a mother?
And this holy child is to be a Savior?

Can my frail body hold heaven's Light!
Let it be according to God's will.
Oh what a Holy night, Holy night.

A palace would have been more suitable
for the birth place of God's Beloved Son.
The miracle of God needs no explanation.

(A Sonnet is a poem with fourteen lines that
uses any of a number of formal rhyme
schemes. In English a sonnet typically has ten
syllables per line.

However all definitions of poetry must be
taken with a grain of salt. Historically, the poet
has been granted freedom to alter syllable
count, rhyme, and rhythm without reason.
Free style poetry is popular today.)

Immanuel

Immanuel means God is with us—
God is in the world and for the world,
in us and for us,
tenderly saving all that can be saved.
We are called to live in God
in ever-widening circles
of faith, hope, and love.

Oh come, Immanuel,
In this fragile vessel to dwell,
link heaven and earth.

The hour is late—
Only love can break
bonds of hate!

The Birth of Jesus

When Jesus was born in the village of Bethlehem in Judea, Herod was king. During this time some wise men from the east came to Jerusalem and said, "Where is the child born to be king of the Jews? We saw his star in the east and have come to worship him." (Matthew 2:1-2, CEV)

When Jesus was born
three wise men came from afar
to welcome His birth.
Bringing gifts of gold,
frankincense, and myrrh.

They kneel before the child
wrapped in swaddling clothes
who outshines all material things.

These earthly gifts were soon depleted.
Yet, Jesus' gentle life
and tender teachings bring,
when sacrificially completed,
enduring love, joy, and peace
for all eternity!

"Behold, the angel of the Lord appeared to Joseph in a dream and said, Rise, take the child and his mother, flee to Egypt, and stay there until I tell you. Herod is going to search for the child to destroy him." (Matthew 2:13)

Joseph's Angel and Herod's Soldiers

When Jesus was born in Bethlehem
Herod's soldiers were riding across the land
killing new-born babies.

Joseph, seized by fear,
took Mary and baby Jesus
to Egypt for safety.

There were no walls
to keep them out for fear of
infesting the land.

At the American Mexican borders and in the Israel-
Hamas war zones, Soldiers ride again.
Stripping babies from mother's arms.

God help us!
Herod's soldiers ride again and again!

Jesus' Birth in the Gospel of Matthew

Into our hate filled world, Jesus comes uninvited.
Comes for all who have no room to lay their head.
Jesus is present for all the poor and homeless.

Gospel of Matthew
The Good News of Jesus' birth
Center of our faith

Mary and baby Jesus
The message of kindness and love
Heaven's approval

Light Dispels Darkness

"The people who sat in darkness have seen a great light, and for those who sat in the region and shadow of death light has dawned." (Matthew 4:16)

God and Jesus as Light
are One in pushing back
the shadow of death.

Star of Bethlehem

Keep shining on our lives

for we are fading

Stone Art

We must construct stone art
to enable it to listen
and speak mysteries to us.

Orpheus charmed animals with his music. His
singing made the trees shiver.
Orpheus even **charmed the stones**.

The Orpheus voice speaks by listening.
Orpheus sees with words coming from inside space.
His seeing invited all creation to join in concertos.

Our stone art expresses, like Orpheus,
this poetic space encompassing all creation.

The beauty and wonder of stone art
is its healing powers
that link possibility with actuality.

Contemplating the beauty of the manger scene
warms our heart with healing love energies.

The Good Shepherd

Psalm 23, The Lord is My Shepherd

When I walk through fields of wild flowers
I know God is my shepherd.
When I wade in gurgling streams
filled with wild salmon
God refreshes my faith in goodness.

When I walk through dark nights,
God is leading me.
God is with me and
I am not afraid.

The Good Shepherd.
makes me feel safe.
Grace fills my cup
until it overflows.

Each day of my life
Kindness
and love are with me.

In God's house of nature
I will live
forever.

"Time to Try the Other Side." (Luke 5:4-6)

Peace Sonnet

Casting net along the Galilean shore,
Shore covered with foam covered stones.
Sea gulls sounding their cry for more.
Peter thinks of the gifts of the waves.

Jesus came and got in my fishing boat,
lifted his arms to heaven and announced,
The crowds are demanding miracles,
It's time to seek solitude on the other side.

I still have much to teach you about love.
I gathered my net and we launched boat.
Jesus laid down in boat, his head on

the balancing rock used as an anchor.
The wind began to fearfully rock the boat.
Jesus said, be still; and all was Peace.

Jesus takes Simon Peter's hand
and keeps him from sinking in the stormy sea.
(See Matthew 14:22-33)

Faith is the road traveled
between earth and heaven—
The lens through which
we view life.

Oh the thrill of sunrise,
like the first dawn of the world.
Walking in dawn's light,
my soul trembles with ecstasy bright.

Without faith
this road we would cease to take.
We would sink
in the storm's wake.

Taking Jesus' hand
we hear, Peace I instill.
God blesses the followers of Jesus
Who walk on this faith road still.

Our mortality is addressed—
Breaking news from immortal lands!
We can face life experiences
taking Jesus' kind hands!

"If any of you want to be my followers,
you must forget about yourself.
You must take up your cross
and follow me." (Mark 8:34)

Walking With Jesus

Walking along the Way,
Jesus called helpers.
Earth and heaven meet.

In Jesus we see God
showing tender care
and goodness.

Faith, the Way traveled
between earth and heaven—
Kindness is the Way.

The thrill of sunrise—
First dawn of new world.
Walking in dawn's light.

My soul trembles
with ecstasy's bright light,
the road we take.

Walking with Jesus
we hear,
Peace, I instill.

    Once you've walked with Jesus—
Taken HIs hand in faith, hope, and love.
    You will never walk alone again.

"Suppose one of you has a hundred sheep and loses one of them. Doesn't he leave the ninety-nine in the open country and go after the lost sheep until he finds it?" (Luke 15:4)

The greatness of Jesus' tender teachings
is that he expressed deep truths
in simple everyday parables.

Oh, seeking Good Shepherd.

God with us and for us.

You seek lost sheep.

Bring them back to sheep-fold.

You shoulder our burden on cross,

To carry us into Glory of God.

Tenderness is Everything

Some mornings
after reading the newspaper,
I feel ashamed at being a human.

The homeless refugees
are asked to stay at home. How
inhumane is this! ?
Take the torch from the hand of the
Statue Lady.

Wipe her tears with her gown.
Remove her crown.

When my heart is breaking
and I can stand no more,
I go for a long walk into the foothills
of the Chugach mountain range.

I sit on a snowy knoll
and watch the alpenglow sunrise unfold.
Gazing at the eternal miracle
that no one can ever ban,
I shed the darkness,
like removing one garment at a time.

The gift of nature,
the tremor of pure sunlight
overcoming exhaustion,
the luminous tender touch we cherish.
The glow of heaven we so need,
the multitudes to seek and feed.

(See my book, *Gentle Galilean Glories: The Tender Teachings of Jesus*, for an explanation of why I use Glory of God instead of Kingdom of God. I show how Glory translates Jesus's message of good news best. Kingdom carries the connotation in our world of dominion and ruling power that is often oppressive.)

"On the day of Pentecost all the Lord's followers were together in one place. Suddenly there was a noise from heaven like the sound of a mighty wind! It filled the house where they were meeting. Then they saw what looked like fiery tongues moving in all directions, and a tongue came and settled on each person there. The Holy Spirit took control of everyone, and they began speaking whatever languages the Spirit let them speak." (Acts 2:1-4)

Pentecost

Candles light the way,

Cherry blossoms in the spring.

Fruit ripened by the sun rays,

Life blazoned by Pentecost light.

Remember with exultation,

in God is our salvation.

*****

When all are hurting
Darkness is in every land
Be someone's candle

Grace Sonnet

The story of creation in the Bible,
a myth with many cultural influences.
You who grace table with bread and wine,
make the myth come true in our time.

You touch us with love so wide and deep,
wake us from our fitful and tossing sleep.
Bring joyful tidings for our soul is sad.
Old man and child, here I hopefully sit,

waiting at the table with candles lit.
Satan's evil spell will finally break,
when the bread from heaven we take.

In covenant Grace at table we dine.
Faithfully we receive the gift of wine.
Miraculously the old myth comes true!

Entering Glory of God

Jesus said, you must become as a little child
to enter into the Glory of God.
(Paraphrase of Matthew 18:3)

A little child sees our cruel world
for the first time, seeing with new eyes.

Border walls topped with razor-wire
Guards marching with assault rifles.

Don't forget the immigrant children,
Jesus loves all children.

The Shape of Love

We				
must	love	when	other	We become
love	comes from	we	each	God's
each other	God	love		children.

Forget-Me-Not Sonnet

I'm an 83-year-old child, Sitting with Jesus.
Eager to learn from the Master Teacher.
I'm humbled without sufficient words.
So many mysteries, waiting like

young birds, to be fed by mother robin.
In every heart there is a child waiting.
Waiting like a song bird to fly for first time.
Jesus says, children, you belong to God.

I am humbled and bow, alleluia!
Sitting as a child listening to Jesus
is truly magical moments in time.

Dear God, may my curiosity flower—
Like Alaska's little, Forget-Me-Nots.
And may I never forget, I am your child.

(The Forget-Me-Not is Alaska's Sate Flower)

"Behold the Lamb of God
who takes away the sins of the world."
(John 1:29)

Oh Lamb of God,
our reminder of the Good Shepherd.

Who sought the lost sheep,
brought them back to sheep-fold.

Shouldering our burden on cross,
To carry us into Glory of God.

And while they were eating,
He said, "Truly I tell you,
one of you will betray Me."

(Matthew 26:21)

In this stone art creation one can see
Judas quietly taking his provocative leave.
What was Judas thinking? Was he frustrated
that Jesus had not become a Messianic deliverer
in the spirit of King David?

Was he trying to provoke Jesus into action?
(See Matthew, chapters 26-28.)

The Lord's Supper portrayed in this stone sculpture is at the heart of this divine drama that links heaven and earth—The bread from heaven that gives life.
(See John 6:48-50)

Banquet Sonnet

We forget that your hands are magical.
You touch wildflowers and they blossom.
You speak of songbirds, and they fly to us.
Your parables let grapes ripen on vine.

The touch of your hands let the blind see,
and let the suffering lame walk again.
Gathering around you on a grassy knoll,
bread loaves are miraculously multiplied.

Fish swim rapidly from hand to hand.
Peace flows from your hand to the multitude.
Love binds all hearts together as one.

When death comes knocking at our door.
The gate of heaven will open, we will hear,
Come my child, the banquet is ready.

Jesus said to him,
"Judas, would you betray
the Son of Man with a kiss?"
(Luke 22:48)

"I have sinned by betraying
a man who has never done
anything wrong."
(Matthew 27:4)

For thirty pieces of silver
Judas betrayed Jesus

Treasurer for the disciples
Judas stole some on the sly

Kind Jesus washed Judas' feet
Humble till the end

Jesus beaten, bled
Crown of thorns on head

Judas could not live with his betrayal
Jesus was a kind friend

"And we are witnesses of all things which he did both in the land of the Jews, and in Jerusalem; whom they slew and hanged on a tree:" (Acts 10:39)

Lenten Gifts

Lent is
a time of stillness

emptying the soul
of noise

There is a sweetness
Hiding in quietness

Desiring
to be shared

We are the vessels
waiting to be filled

Gifts from heaven
Life eternal

Jesus pours the wine
Breaks the bread

Come to the Lenten table
Where all are fed

Come to the Supper
Never a feast was finer
Eat, drink, and live
Anger and darkness be gone
Let charity light the world

"If I be lifted up, I will draw all persons to me."
(John 12:32)

I
w
i
l
l
when I am lifted up on cross

d
r
a
w

a
l
l

p
e
o
p
l
e

Power of Sacrificial Love

Jesus is lifted up on the cross

Love lifted me

Jesus' prayer from cross

The fragrance violets send out

on the heels that crush

I see the cross

I don't understand it

I know what it's about

Cosmic healing love

Crucifixion Sonnet

You woke me from a fitful fearful sleep.
Spells were broken, I did joyfully weep.
The story is light coming from the stones.
In that radiant light all my fear is gone.

You walked willfully toward the cross,
and love was triumphant over loss.
Dear Jesus, help me share your stories
and follow your Galilean glories.

Denying self and worldly power—
As Comforter you come to ease our pain.
Over the power of evil you reign.

Relying on persuasive love, you lure.
With relational kind words that cure.
I will take up my cross and share your love.

"I told you the most important part of the message exactly as it was told to me. That part is: Christ died for our sins, as the scriptures say. He was buried, and three days later he was raised to life." (I Corinthians 15:3-4, CEV)

Cross and Resurrection in New Testament

I walk in nature
Shadow of cross falls on path
Sadness grips my heart

A snowshoe hare squalls
All of Nature is weeping
Lynx with food for kits

Searching for meaning
Stained with bloodshed and travail
Grief of centuries fall

Pain of families
From loss of children in war
Sadness rings in ears

Look up at the sky
Blazing in glory for all
God's light shines

Searching for meaning in life
I crave beauty and goodness
Yet haunted by loss

Who told the geese
It was time to take wing and fly
Opening magic vistas

The Voice that told the geese
It was time to go— Speaks to us
Bringing hope of new victories

Lift your eyes to the cross
Doors open new revelations
of sacrificial Love

Lent and Easter

In this time of pandemic,
our lives; and indeed our world,
is experiencing great sorrow.

Silence is the sound of sorrow—
The voice of mourning.
The stone is rolled, sealing the tomb.

Out of the silence of Lent,
comes the Easter song—
He is risen! He is risen, indeed!

The Church will survive
only if it can regain this clear message
for the suffering wayfaring crowds:

God so loved the world—
Love incarnated in tender teachings.
Healing brokenness, saving all.

The Crucified Jesus—
Body was placed in a tomb.
Stone was rolled to seal grave.

On Easter morning—
Stone was rolled away
Jesus is risen!

"They were looking intently up into the sky as he was going, when suddenly two men dressed in white stood beside them. 'Men of Galilee, they said, 'why do you stand here looking into the sky? This same Jesus, who has been taken from you into heaven, will come back in the same way you have seen him go into heaven.'" (Acts 1:10-11)

Stone art reveals God
A miraculous revelation
Heaven beckons

Jesus the incarnate Word
is lifted into heaven
Transformed he comes back
into the lives of his followers
Becomes a compassionate companion
Who understands suffering

Memories of Jesus'
Gentle Galilean Glories
Live forever

The meaning of Jesus as Living Word of God
is always eluding us. Human words fail
when we try to talk about this essence.
Poetry is a search for the connection,
God and Jesus as One.

In Jesus God the Poet is speaking
living words that enrich the soul.
Like fruit ripening in the summer sun—
Enriching permanence of the soul.

Faith Sonnet

I miss my mother and dad at the helm
I miss my four sisters and three brothers
who now reside in heaven's bright realm.
Heaven is not measured in miles,

It is not far away, but is near to us
in our soul's imagination and smiles.
The kindness that is partial in us
Is all-embracing in kindness of God.

In Jesus' words heaven came very near.
After his sacrificial death on the cross
Jesus was lifted into heaven's glory.

Transformed he returns as Comforter.
Saying to all his faithful followers,
On this Rock of faith, I will build my Church.

"Here I am! I stand at the door and Knock. If anyone hears my voice and opens the door, I will come in and eat with that person, and they with me." (Rev. 3:20, NIV)

Behold, I stand at the door and knock

According to Revelation 1:11, on the Greek island of Patmos, the risen Jesus instructs John of Patmos to: "Write what you see and send it to the seven Churches: Ephesus, Smyrna, Pergamum, Thyatira, Sardis, Philadelphia, and Laodicea."

The Church of Laodicea was a Church with a lukewarm faith. Laodicea was a prosperous commercial center. They allowed economic prosperity to cause spiritual bankruptcy. Those in Laodicea's church who open the door to the risen Jesus will share in His Heavenly banquet and have the right to sit with Him on His throne.

Go away!
You can't come in.
The door is securely locked.
I do not know you. I am staying safe.
The world is shaking.

I will build your house on stone, a solid foundation.

I've hidden my talents. I'm kidding under covers.
Who is at the door, singing my name?

Love chimes—

"I pray that you will be blessed
with kindness and peace from God,
who is and was, and is coming.

May you receive kindness and
peace . . . before the throne of God."
(Revelation 1:4, CEV)

"May Jesus be kind to all of you."
(Revelation 22:21, CEV)

In poetic language,
This is John's message—

Hello God,
A vision came to me.
This is what I saw:
People suffering.
Praying, how long, God.

Words were spoken.
Inspiring songs were sung.
Jesus will be kind to you.

John's vision—
A new heaven and new earth.
Comes by kindness and peace.

Lord Jesus come.
Be kind to everyone.
World without end.

Love Sonnet

God, our world is big, our love so small.

Does our drop of love matter at all?

Are we play acting on a bigger stage?

Adding our sculpture and poems on page?

Go away. We want to write the script.

Love only the ones like us on the stage.

The love that is so small in our actions

Is all-embracing in your covenant passion.

Let your love break through our darkness

Filling our lives with heaven's brightness.

Heal our lives with your loving kindness.

Join us as one with all your children.

Doubt knock's constantly at our door.

Come in, we believe, help our unbelief!

Lessons Learned from Stone Art

Each generation
Has doubts as to the meaning
of faith and practice

Stone art portraying
The tender teachings of Jesus
Teach valuable lessons

Give a foundation
to our Christian faith
and practice

Giving attention
to the permanent truths
that shape our lives

1. Stone art speaks patience—

    Ripples in the stream
    whisper messages as the water flows
    over stones and around larger rocks.

    Mated harlequins sitting on a rock
    are attuned to the soft music,
    watching for flashes of rainbows.

    I stand in awe of their patience.
    Soothed by the soft music.
    Heart pounding with gratitude!

    Thank you,
    for teaching me to be patient—
    Receive the gift of inner peace.

2. Stone art teaches contemplation—

    "Be Still and Know that I am God." (Isaiah 46:10) When life is confusing and you're feeling depressed, how can you "be still" and "know" what to do?

a. Identify the problem causing the depression. What is it that is weighing you down? Why do you feel the need to "be still"?

b. Identify your anxiety. What is at the root of your fear?

c. Having identified your anxiety, consider that life responsibilities sometimes require you to step into roles and do the very thing you fear the most.

Is your conscience calling you to take the step that you fear to take?

Many of our models of the past like Isaiah, Jesus, and Mother Teresa stepped into challenging roles after quiet times of meditation. They discovered God's promise of presence that gave them strength to act.

God gave them a spirit of kindness. The ekphrastic stone poems in this book are born in contemplation of scenes from the life of Jesus.

Ekphrastic Nature Poetry

Ekphrastic poetry
at its best is born
in contemplation of nature.

Seeing first what is actually
there in the stone art observed
and what the observed signifies,
not in what the observed
can be made to signify.

Poetry seeks a self-consistent
understanding of things observed
and adapts appearance to reality
in the pursuit of truth,
beauty, and goodness.

If one has eyes to see,
a mystery can be discovered in all of nature.
A little humor is good,
but the seeing must be honest.

God, weaving of the world
into God's eternal nature,
fills the world with kindness
and all glow with the light of heaven.

The sky and seas
The mountains and trees
The birds, flowers, and bees,
and our own lives.

In contemplating stone art
Mystery dances in the music
the garden composes.
Poetry hears this music
and pens the notes.

The mystic and poet
become one as the symphony
is played and heard.
Glory to the lover
hidden in nature's beauty.

This maxim is true—
stone art is the poem.

3. Stone art teaches the importance of silence—

Out of the silence of Lent,
comes the Easter song—
He is risen! He is risen, indeed!

Oh how beautifully
Stone sculptures
Invite stillness
Be still and know

4. Stone art teaches gratitude—

> Stone art teaches me to stand in awe.
> Soothed by music of angels.
> Heart pounding with gratitude!

5. Stone art teaches adventure—

> Stone art is an adventure
> Opening the mystery of the centuries
> Revealing truth, beauty, and love.

6. Stone art teaches joy—

> Observing stone art
> Inspires joyful soul music
> Angels singing

7. Stone art teaches openness with all things—

> Stones are never isolated, but are connected with everything that is before them, beside them, under them, and over them. Stones both clothe and reveal the spirit of nature. Stones have centuries compressed in them. A stone poem is nature magically revealing itself.

8. Stone art teaches Beauty—

One purpose of this book has been to discover beauty. One test of beauty is does it contribute to a more beautiful society?

Does it make people stronger in their resolve to build a more beautiful world? Does beauty result in goodness and kindness—The purpose and end of art, especially poetry.

A Summary Vision of Beauty

My vision for the world is that it move toward Beauty. Seeing Beauty in stone art is a step in that direction.

Beauty is the key for understanding
the loving and generous heart beat of nature.

The inner nourishing of a kind spirit in every person is one of the most important needs in our world today.

Beauty in one's heart is felt by the universe.

Yet, I am painfully aware of the chasm between this vision and its ultimate expression in our world that is so divided.

Visions may be expressed in gentle words, but they are more powerful when expressed in tender actions.

Centered in Beauty and Kindness
We can transform our world.

9. Stone art teaches Kindness—

> May kindness be in our thoughts,
> making them good and loving.
> May kindness be in our eyes,
> leading us to see what is just in life.
>
> May kindness be in our hands and feet
> so that we may be of service to others.
> May kindness be in our whole being.
>
> Making us one with God,
> one with all people,
> and one with the universe.
>
> > Stone sculptures speak kindness
> > Gather the light of heaven
> > Warm all in its glow

10. Stone art teaches power of creative imagination—

> Spending time quietly observing art
> sharpens one's imaginative powers,
> leading the way to seeing with new eyes
> and hearing symphonies when stones speak

11. Stone art teaches value for self and all others—

> William Wordsworth spent his life walking in the beauty of nature. HIs longest poem, "The Prelude," closes with this autobiographical reflection: I have learned value for myself and value for all others.

12. Stone art nurtures the soul—

> Stone art,
> nurtures the soul,
> leading to an inclusive love of all humankind.
>
> This soul nurturing
> in beauty and goodness leads to kindness
> in communal living.
>
> The prophets of Old Testament times:
> Isaiah and Hosea were nurtured
> in the covenant grace of kindness.
> Jesus shook hands with these prophets.
>
> Carried their teachings to a new level of
> inclusive and relational tenderness
> in his Gentle Galilean Glories.

13. Stone art teaches healing—

> Harvard professor, E. O. Wilson, biologists, ecologist, entomologist, and naturalist, said prior to his death in 2021, that we need to speak in a clear voice, using science and the humanities, to bring the hope of healing for our hurting world. The poems in this book seek to fulfill that challenge.
>
> God so loved the world—
> Love incarnated in tender teachings.
> Healing brokenness, saving all.
>
> *When Stones Speak* our soul is revitalized
> Heaven comes down.

Healing Stone Art

Orpheus charmed animals with his music.
His singing made the trees shiver.
Orpheus even charmed the stones.

The Orpheus voice speaks by listening.
He sees with words coming from inside
space. His seeing invited all creation to join
in concertos.

Our stone art expresses this poetic space
encompassing all creation.

We must construct stone art to enable it to
listen and speak mysteries to us.

The beauty and wonder of stone art
is its healing powers
that link possibility with actuality.
Contemplating the beauty
of the manger scene warms our heart
with healing love energies.

14. Stone art teaches faith, hope, and love—

> Stone poems
> Speak faith, hope, and love
> Keep doubts away
>
> Putting life in focus
> One stone sculpture at a time

Poems of faith, hope, love

15. Stone art teaches the Spirit of Wonder—

> Wonder shaped into reality.
> Rainbow colors
> Translucent sunlight
> Heaven's light
> Bouncing in polished stones
>
> Art begins in Wonder,
> and when it has done its best
> art ends in Wonder.

16. Stone art teaches Peace—

Peace Sonnet

> Jesus standing with outstretched arms,
> the boat comes peacefully to the shore.
> A quiet center within the raging storm.
> Booming thunder is sounding no more.
> Now the disciples are more afraid
> than they were during the storm's chill.
> Who is this man who can walk on water
> and command the waves to be still?
> God walking in the world, loving the world.
> God in us and for us, tenderly luring.
> Saving all that can be saved from loss.
> The Peace that passes all understanding.
> Mending broken hearts, kindness to all.
> The gracious gift of immortality!

Conclusion

"Let the beauty we love be what we do. There are hundreds of ways to kneel and kiss the ground."
—Rumi

These stone sculptures and poems
have been baptized in science, process philosophy, theology, and code breaking genetic research. God is seen with new eyes as the Poet of the World luring us toward Beauty and Wonder. We invite you to continue with us on this adventurous journey.

Robert crossed a stream
A stone shining with sunlight
Caught his imagination
The stone started to speak
I contain great wisdom
Robert sat on a larger rock
Heard the stone whisper
You are not alone
The hermit thrush sang
Robert smiled deeply

Stone Art

This stone art has been constructed
to enable us to listen
and speak mysteries.

The Orpheus voice speaks by listening.
Orpheus sees with words coming from inside space.
His seeing invited all creation to join in concertos.

Our stone art expresses
this poetic space encompassing all creation.

The beauty and wonder of stone art
is its healing powers
that link possibility with actuality.

Contemplating the beauty of gentle teachings
warms our heart with healing love energies.

I would like a table, please.

Bread and wine for everyone.

For my friends, Abraham, MLK,

John, Bobby. Pens to write about

freedom.

Another essential table
for Plato, Jesus, Einstein, and Whitehead.
All other tables are footnotes to this one.
This is a heavenly banquet.
The sky shines with stars.

      Let us go out now
      Become a heavenly light
      In someone's darkness

Kindness Sonnet

Jesus, friend of the weak and suffering,
only you understand my daily needs.
In my weakness I count it a blessing
that only you know my everyday deeds.

My collective unconscious is dark.
My shadow thoughts are tearing me apart
My personal consciousness is my voice.
Help me always make the right choice.

My free will seems to have escaped me,
and my genes decide without asking me.
So come, Risen Jesus, and be my Friend.

I will be your disciple to the end.
Daily transformed by your kindness,
I will be kind to all of your children.

(This sonnet is shaped by the tender
teachings of Jesus, the in-depth psychology of
Carl Jung, and code breaking genetic research).

> Tired and feeling sad?
> Sit beside these rock sculptures.
> Let the centuries speak to you.
> Discover hidden gems in rocks.
> Find peace in your soul.

APPENDIX I, JESUS IS KIND

Ten Key Biblical Verses that support the thesis of these poems that Jesus was kind and that his teachings were tender

1. "God's love and **kindness** will shine upon us like the sun that rises in the sky. On us who live in the dark shadow of death, this light will shine to guide us into a life of peace." (Luke 1:78-79)

2. Jesus said, "Come to me, all of you who are tired from carrying heavy loads, and I will give your rest. Take my yoke and put it on you, and learn from me, because I am **gentle and humble in spirit**; and you will find rest. For the yoke I will give you is easy and the load I will put on you is light." (Matthew 11:28-30)

3. Jesus said, "Blessed are the gentle, they will receive what God has promised!" (Matthew 5:5)

4. Jesus taught, "People who are well do not need a doctor, but only those who are sick. Go and find out what is meant by the scripture that says, 'It is **kindness** that I want, not animal sacrifices.' I have not come to call respectable people, but outcasts." (Matthew 9:12-13)

5. "A man with leprosy came to Jesus and knelt down. **Jesus felt sorry for him** so he put his hands on him and said, 'You are well.'" (Mark 1:40-41)

6. "Jesus said, "Don't worry about your life. **God will take care of you**." (Luke 12:22-26)

7. Paul in imitating the spirit of Jesus, grounds kindness in the being of God, "You are God's people so **be gentle, kind, humble, and meek**." (Colossians 3:12)

8. "**Be kind and merciful**, and forgive others, just as God forgave you because of Jesus." (Ephesians 4:32).

9. "I pray that you will **be blessed with kindness** and peace from God, who is and was and is coming. May you receive kindness and peace from Jesus, the faithful witness." (Revelation 1:4-5).

10. "I pray that **Jesus will be kind to all of you**." (Revelation 22:21).

> May kindness be in our thoughts,
> making them good and loving.
> May kindness be in our eyes,
> leading us to see what is just in life.
>
> May kindness be in our hands and feet
> so that we may be of service to others.
> May kindness be in our whole being.
>
> Making us one with God,
> one with all people,
> and one with the universe.

APPENDIX II, GOD AS RELATIONAL KINDNESS

God as relational kindness, is the lens through which the poems in this book are written. A key biblical verse is—*"God, you brought me safely through birth, and you protected me as a baby at my mother's breast. From the day I was born I have been in your tender care, and from my birth you have been by my side."* (Author's paraphrase of Psalm 22:9-10)

When centered in God's creative loving kindness we live and move and have our being in a circle of kindness that takes in the whole world. God is in all entities and for all, in the world and for the world. Jesus was responsive to God's love aims and purposes for his life and became more God conscious with each self-actualization. Jesus' God consciousness, the very real existence of God in Jesus, enabled him to be more conscious of the needs of others in an ever widening circle of loving kindness, and thus more fully divine and human.

Jesus spoke to God as a child would speak to a parent, confidently and securely. Jesus saw God like a kind father and nurturing mother.

> The biblical image of faith in the time of Jesus was of a child wrapped in the folds of a mother's garment where there is security, comfort, nurturing, love, kindness, and hope.

God's loving kindness involves God as present in the world. True kindness feels what the other person is feeling, rejoicing in their joys and hurting with their pains. We would doubt that a husband loves his wife if he were not aware of her feelings and if his feelings did not reflect her feelings and respond with kindness.

As we experience God revealed in Jesus, we find God rejoicing with us in our times of joy and weeping with us in our times of sorrow. Our kindness toward others is based on this responsive kindness we see in God. Our stone art reflects the awe and wonder of God being in the world, in us, and for us, holding us close as a mother wraps her child in the folds of her garments or tenderly holds her child in her lap.

The God we meet in the beauty of stone art is in us and for us. The beauty of the stone art reflects the goodness, grace, beauty, and kindness of God. God is tenderly present in all things.

The call of God toward kindness seen in Jesus' tender teachings is a call to all people. (See my book, *Gentle Galilean Glories: The Tender Teachings of Jesus*). For Christians, Jesus is the supreme example of loving kindness. To affirm this does not lessen the role of Moses for Judaism, Mohammed for Islam or Buddha for Buddhism, and other important religious teachers. Buddha said often, "My religion is kindness."

When any one relates to the God of creative possibilities, creative transformation occurs, bringing harmony and peace.

God's loving kindness is persuasive and luring, not coercive and demanding. Relational kindness does not seek to control with coercion. Relational power is greatest in its ability to influence others. If we love someone we do not seek to control or pressure them with promises and threats. Instead we try to persuade them with tender luring love to actualize the possibilities for goodness, beauty, and kindness. The gentle Galilean glories of Jesus define power in terms of loving kindness.

God as relational kindness is a vision that can change our world into one community knitted together by kind words and gentle loving actions. (For a more complete development of a relational hermeneutic of kindness see my book, *A Relational Hermeneutic of Kindness*). This hope filled vision taps into the healing energy of kindness found in most religions and makes it the prism through which we understand God, the world, and all things. Kindness is the language known around the world.

The list of my books on the next page were all born from my masters thesis, HERMENEUTICAL THEORY IN TRANSITION AS REFLECTED IN INTERPRETATION: A JOURNAL OF BIBLE AND THEOLOGY (1947-1966); and my doctoral dissertation, BAPTISM AND THE LORD'S SUPPER IN THE GOSPEL OF JOHN: A HERMENEUTICAL INQUIRY. This parentage is especially true of my book, *A Relational Hermeneutic of Kindness.* On the deepest level, all of my 50-year preaching ministry, published articles, Sunday School lessons, and devotions were born from this parentage and nurtured in God's relational kindness. My poetry books for the last decade have especially sought to unite science and the humanities in one clear voice that brings healing and transformation. Relational theology sees God in the world and for the world, in us and for us. In this relational kindness people of all sexualities, gender identities and expressions are equally loved by God and are an integral part of God's diverse family. God calls all persons, and all who respond become co-workers with God's novel aims and purposes.

**Dwayne Cole** and his wife, Beth met while they were both in seminary studying for the Master of Divinity degree. Dwayne has also earned a Master of Theology and a Ph.D. in New Testament with a major in Greek. They have an adult son and daughter and four grandchildren. They moved to Alaska in 2011 to be with family. Their daughter and son-in- law came to start their medical practice and needed help with their two children. Dwayne's passion is poetry that is inspired by his daily walks in the beauty and wonder of Alaska.

BOOKS BY DWAYNE COLE

A Center that Holds: Adventures in Kindness
Alpenglow Miracles: Fire Dance of Wonder
A Prayer of Blessing:
As You Go Remember This
A Relational Hermeneutic of Kindness
A Relational Trinity of Kindness
BEARS AND MOOSE OF ALASKA: Nature Poetry
Clouds of Inspiration
Down on the Farm in Georgia: A Poetic Memoir
Dragonfly Magic
Gentle Galilean Glories: The Tender Teachings of Jesus
God and Evil: An Ode to Kindness
Heart Haiku: Alaska Inspired Photos and Poems
Heart Sijo: Alaska Inspired Photos and Poems
Jesus' Transforming Beatitudes: Selected Sermons from Year A
Jesus' Transforming Love: Selected Sermons from Year B
Jesus' Transforming Gentle Teachings: Selected Sermons from Year C

Kindness Is Every Step
Lone Leaf Dancing
Poems Inspired by Process Philosophy
Poet of the Universe: A Vision of Beauty and Goodness.
Rainbows of Hope
Snowshoe Hare Beauty
The Apostles' Creed: A Living Creed for the Living Church
The Bible: A Poetic Journey
The Book of Revelation: Jesus' Kindness Transforms Suffering
The Serenity Prayer: A Pathway to Peace and Happiness
*The Story of the Bible: Authority, Inspiration, Canonization,
     and Translation*
TREES AND DRIFTWOOD: Poetic Ecology
When Flowers Speak, Listen
When Stones Speak
WINGS OF INSPIRATION

 **Bob Watkins** and his wife Marji live in Iowa. He currently works in church relations for Bethel University, where he earned a B. S. in Biology and later received a Master of Divinity and Doctor of Ministry from Vanderbilt University. Marji and Bob have 5 children. Bob is a writer. His great passion has been the Great Commission of Jesus--"You shall be my witnesses in Jerusalem, Judea, Samaria, and to the ends of the earth."

Each sculpture featured in this book is representative of the hundreds of pieces Dr. Watkins has created over the last ten years. They vary in size from 3" x 3" x 3" to 16" x 16" x 16".

Many of the works in this book are already sold, but if a follower is drawn to a particular theme or style, please send him an email at watkr@mac.com and he will send you details along with the price of a similar piece that can be commissioned or purchased from the inventory at the time.

Books by Robert Watkins

These Are My Witnesses (1993). *Out of print.*
God's Mighty Acts around the Globe (2013)
God's Mighty Acts around the Globe – A Study Guide (2014)
Chasing Rainbows (2015)
Obedience a Personal Choice (2018)
Fields—From the Fields of the Midwest to the Fields of the World (2021)

www.ingramcontent.com/pod-product-compliance
Lightning Source LLC
LaVergne TN
LVHW052138280525
812433LV00017B/710